Seasons

Winter

Siân Smith

Heinemann Library
Chicago, Illinois

Editorial: Rebecca Rissman, Charlotte Guillain, and Siân Smith
Picture research: Elizabeth Alexander and Sally Claxton
Designed by Joanna Hinton-Malivoire
Printed and bound by South China Printing Company Limited

13 12 11 10 09
10 9 8 7 6 5 4 3 2 1

ISBN-13: 978-1-4329-2730-1 (hc)
ISBN-13: 978-1-4329-2735-6 (pb)

Library of Congress Cataloging-in-Publication Data
Smith, Siân.
  Winter / Siân Smith.
      p. cm. -- (Seasons)
  Includes bibliographical references and index.
  1. Winter--Juvenile literature. I. Title.
  QB637.8.S65 2008
  508.2--dc22
                                              2008049162

Acknowledgments
The author and publisher are grateful to the following for permission to reproduce copyright material:
©Alamy pp.**8** (David R Frazier Photolibrary, Inc.), **20** (Gay Bumgarne), **7** (Ian Francis), **12** (Iconotec), **10** (Image Source Black), **13**, **23 middle** (Pamela Osinski), **19** (Pawel Libera), **18**, **23 top** (Profimedia International s.r.o.), **21** (WILDLIFE GmbH); ©Corbis pp.**14** (Ariel Skelley), **04 br** (Image100), **16** (Tom Stewart), **17** (Veer/Fancy), **11** (Visions of America/Joseph Sohm), **04 tl** (Zefa/Roman Flury); ©GAP Photos p.**22** (J S Sira); ©Getty Images p.**04 tr** (Floria Werner); ©iStockphoto.com pp.**6, 23 bottom** (Bojan Tezak), **04 bl** (Inga Ivanova); ©PhotoDisc. 1999 p.**9** (Steve Mason); ©Photolibrary p.**5** (Pritz Pritz); © Shutterstock **p.15** (Csaba Peterdi).
Cover photograph reproduced with permission of ©Corbis (Craig Tuttle). Back cover photograph reproduced with permission of ©Alamy (WILDLIFE GmbH).

Every effort has been made to contact copyright holders of any material reproduced in this book. Any omissions will be rectified in subsequent printings if notice is given to the publisher.

Contents

What Is Winter?

spring

summer

fall

winter

There are four seasons every year.

Winter is one of the four seasons.

When Is Winter?

spring

summer

winter

fall

The four seasons follow a pattern.

Winter comes after fall.

The Weather in Winter

It can be cold in winter.

It can snow in winter.

What Can We See in Winter?

In winter we can see people in gloves.

In winter we can see people in coats.

In winter we can see trees with
no leaves.

In winter we can see ice.

In winter we can see sleds.

In winter we can see skaters.

In winter we can see snowmen.

In winter we can see hot drinks.

In winter we can see decorations.

In winter we can see lights.

In winter some birds are hungry.

In winter some animals are sleeping.

Which Season Comes Next?

Which season comes after winter?

Picture Glossary

 **decoration** something used to make things look good

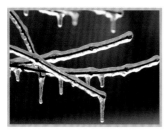 **ice** frozen water. Ice can be cold, hard, and slippery.

 **pattern** happening in the same order

Index

Note to Parents and Teachers
Before reading
Talk to the children about the four seasons of the year: spring, summer, fall, and winter. Ask the children in which season do we celebrate Thanksgiving? In which season do we observe Memorial Day? In which season do we start the New Year? In which season is the weather the hottest?

After reading
Make a puppet snowman. Cut a snowman outline (three connected circles) out of white paper. Cut a hat, two eyes and three buttons out of black paper. Cut a nose out of orange paper. Help children to stick the shapes on the snowman outline.

Create a snowy scene. Help children draw a snowy scene on white paper using colorless wax crayons. Paint over the scene with white paint. The paint will not cover the crayon and will give the effect of snow covering the ground. While the paint is still wet, scatter white or silver glitter.